STATE GUIDES

HISTORIC MONUMENTS

Linden McNeilly

Rourke
Educational Media

rourkeeducationalmedia.com

★★★★★★★★ Introduction ★★★★★★★★

Historic sites and monuments are important places in the United States. Memorable things—some good and some terrible—have happened in history at national sites and landmarks. National historic monuments are especially beautiful, scientifically interesting, or may contain evidence of earlier life.

The Antiquities Act of 1906 gave the president the right to designate national monuments. National historic landmarks and sites are designated by the United States Secretary of the Interior. Congress can also designate national historic sites.

Protecting the past helps us remember our triumphs and learn from our mistakes. This book contains only a few of the hundreds of sites where meaningful things happened. All of them are part of America's national story.

★★★★★★★★ Contents ★★★★★★★★

ALABAMA 4

ALASKA 5

ARIZONA.....................6

ARKANSAS 7

CALIFORNIA 8

COLORADO 9

CONNECTICUT 10

DELAWARE 11

FLORIDA 12

GEORGIA 13

HAWAII.....................14

IDAHO 15

ILLINOIS.....................16

INDIANA 16

IOWA.....................17

KANSAS.....................18

KENTUCKY.....................19

LOUISIANA 20

MAINE 21

MARYLAND 22

MASSACHUSETTS 22

MICHIGAN.....................23

MINNESOTA 24

MISSISSIPPI 25

MISSOURI 26

MONTANA 26

NEBRASKA.....................27

NEVADA 28

NEW HAMPSHIRE 29

NEW JERSEY 30

NEW MEXICO 31

NEW YORK 32

NORTH CAROLINA.....................32

NORTH DAKOTA 33

OHIO 34

OKLAHOMA 35

OREGON 36

PENNSYLVANIA 36

RHODE ISLAND.....................37

SOUTH CAROLINA 38

SOUTH DAKOTA.....................38

TENNESSEE.....................39

TEXAS 40

UTAH 41

VERMONT.....................42

VIRGINIA 43

WASHINGTON.....................44

WASHINGTON, D.C. 45

WEST VIRGINIA 46

WISCONSIN.....................46

WYOMING.....................47

INDEX 48

Brown Chapel AME Church, National Historic Landmark

In March of 1965, organizers worked here to resist racism. When 600 protestors marched from Selma to the capital on March 7, 1965, police attacked them. But TV coverage of the brutality drew more support for the marchers, turning the tide in their favor.

On March 21, 1965, 3,200 marchers began a 70 mile (112.65 kilometer) walk to Montgomery. At the capitol four days later, they were 25,000-strong. President Johnson signed the Voting Rights Act five months later.

Location:	Established:
Selma, AL	1982

Alaska

Admiralty Island National Monument

Admiralty Island is part of Tongass National Forest in the Alaska Panhandle. Its large population of grizzly, black, and brown bears makes it a rare, pristine place. This area is also home to whales, mountain goats, and deer.

Bears outnumber people here, but there are more bald eagles than bears. There are more bald eagles here than in the remainder of the United States! Tlingit Indians, descendants of the tribes that have controlled the Straits for centuries, make up the only permanent community.

Location:	Established:
Admiralty Island, AK	1978

Canyon de Chelly National Monument

Located in northeastern Arizona and within the Navajo Nation, this impressive canyon comprises 84,000 acres (33,993.6 hectares). Its colorful sheer cliffs, rivers, and cliff dwellings are stunning and culturally significant.

People have lived continuously on the Colorado Plateau for nearly 5,000 years. Navajo families still live and farm the lands. The National Park Service and Navajo Nation work together to manage Canyon de Chelly.

Location:	Established:
Chinle, AZ	1931

Little Rock Central High School
National Historic Site

After the Supreme Court deemed segregation illegal, Little Rock Central High School was the place it became real. With National Guard protection, nine African-American students enrolled in the formerly all-white school in the fall of 1957, beginning a wave of desegregation.

These teenagers, ages 15 to 17, faced cruelty and angry mobs. Today they are referred to as the "Little Rock Nine," and are considered civil rights activists for their bravery in the face of great obstacles.

Location:	Established:
Little Rock, AR	1998

Manzanar National Historic Site

During World War II, the United States government ordered Japanese-American citizens and resident Japanese immigrants to relocation camps. Most of those at Manzanar were American citizens. They lived in prison-like conditions. It was dusty and sweltering in the summer, and below freezing in the winter.

Internees established schools, churches, and clubs. They offered sports, music, and community programs such as working on the newspaper and in the gardens. More than ten thousand people were forced to live at Manzanar from 1942–1945.

Location:	Established:
Independence, CA	1992

Sand Creek Massacre National Historic Site

In November of 1864 the U.S. Cavalry attacked a peaceful Cheyenne and Arapaho settlement. At first, the soldiers called the conflict a "battle." But eyewitnesses soon painted a brutal picture of massacre, with most of the victims being women, children, and elderly men.

Captain Silas Soule and Lieutenant Joseph A. Cramer refused to order their men to participate, and later gave evidence about the horrors to the authorities. Soule was shot on the street a few weeks after revealing the truth of the massacre. His murderer was not charged.

Location:	Established:
Chivington, CO	2007

Weir Farm National Historic Site

This farm's purpose is the preservation of art and beauty. Three generations have lived and worked here, painting, drawing, and etching the natural world, using the landscape and buildings as both inspiration and retreat.

Julian Weir traded a painting and $10 with collector Erwin Davis for the 153-acre (61.92 hectare) farm. Weir and his wife, Anna Baker, had three children. A year after Anna died in childbirth, Julian married her sister, Ella, who had helped raise the three daughters.

Location:	Established:
Wilton, CT	1990

Delaware

★ ★ ★ ★ ★ ★ ★ ★ ★

New Castle Courthouse Museum
National Historic Landmark

This was the site of a famous abolitionist trial and a stop on the Underground Railroad. Originally built in 1680, then rebuilt in 1732, founders established Delaware as an independent state here. It is one of the oldest courthouses in the United States.

Thomas Garrett and fellow abolitionist John Hunn helped slaves escape, violating the Fugitive Slave Act of 1793. Found guilty, they paid fines and lost homes and property. Even still, Garrett promised publicly to continue to help those oppressed by slavery regardless of the cost.

Location:	Established:
New Castle, DE	1972

Florida

★ ★ ★ ★ ★ ★ ★ ★   ★ ★ ★ ★ ★ ★ ★ ★

Castillo de San Marcos National Monument

Built in 1672, this fort served under four flags. Under Spanish command, it defended against British sieges. Under the British, it held off American revolutionaries. Later, it flew the Confederate flag. The United States defended the fort during the Seminole and Spanish-American Wars.

In 1767, Dr. Andrew Turnbull recruited 1,403 Mediterranean people to work his indigo fields. So many of them died of mistreatment and disease that survivor's walked 70 miles (112.65 kilometers) to the fort to plead for protection. Their descendants populate the town today.

Location:	Established:
St. Augustine, FL	1924

Ocmulgee National Monument

Ocmulgee National Monument is an important prehistoric American Indian site. American Indians hunted Ice Age mammals during the Paleo-Indian period. They occupied this land for thousands of years, leaving artifacts such as the remains of canoes, fabric, tools, and housing settlements.

William McIntosh ("White Warrior") was a Creek Nation chief in the early 19th century. He was a successful businessman, and he owned slaves. His power came from his mother's side, the Wind Clan. But that didn't save him when his tribe ordered his death after he signed a treaty they disagreed with.

Location:	Established:
Macon, GA	1936

Papahanaumokua Kea Marine National Monument

This incredible tract of land is home to over 7,000 marine species and seabirds, including the threatened green turtle, the endangered Hawaiian monk seal, and the world's most endangered duck, the Laysan duck. It's 139,797 square miles (362,073 square kilometers), larger than all the country's national parks combined.

A whaler, *Parker*, sank here in 1842. Survivors fashioned a raft and made it ashore, where they survived on marine life and the remains of another shipwreck. They tied wood sticks with messages to seabirds' legs to plea for help. They were rescued after eight months.

Location:	Established:
Honolulu, HI	2006

Idaho

Hagerman Horse Fossil Beds National Monument

In 1928, a local rancher found fossil bones that turned out to be the first evidence of an ancient single-toed horse. More than 20 complete horse skeletons and tens of thousands of fossils have been found. This area contains the largest concentration of Hagerman horse fossils in North America.

This site is internationally significant due to pre Ice-Age fossils from 3.5 million years ago, which is the earliest appearance of modern plants and animals. Species found include mastodons, dirk tooth cats, and bone crushing dogs.

Location:	Established:
Hagerman, ID	1988

Pullman National Monument

Pullman was the first planned industrial community housing workers for Pullman, a railroad car manufacturer. It was the scene of the violent 1894 Pullman strike. The site includes the Pullman factory, Hotel Florence, and the A. Philip Randolph Pullman Porter Museum.

Long-distance train travel required sleeping cars and porters, who were mostly African American. A. Philip Randolph founded their worker's union in 1925. Forty-four percent of the Pullman workforce was porters, making Pullman the nation's largest employer of African Americans.

Location:	Established:
Chicago, IL	2015

Indiana

Duck Creek Aqueduct National Historic Landmark

Built around 1846, the Duck Creek Aqueduct is the only surviving covered wood aqueduct in the United States. It's part of the American canal system, hand-dug waterways that were used with

(Indiana continued)

drafting animals walking alongside and pulling with a rope.

Canal transportation worked best for large, heavy loads that would move even more slowly in carts. When it was no longer needed, the waterways were used for mills.

Location:	Established:
Metamora, IN	2014

 Iowa

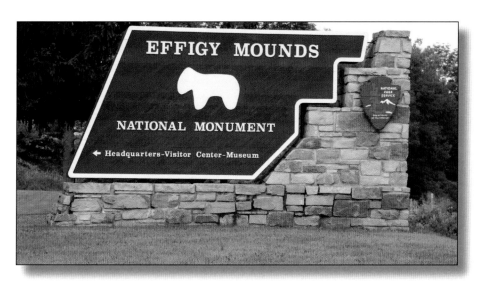

Effigy Mounds National Monument

About 1,400 years ago, American Indians known as the Effigy Moundbuilders built unusual mounds along the picturesque Upper Mississippi River. Each regional group favored certain shapes of animals such as lynx, birds, bears, and bison.

The exact reason for the mounds is a mystery. The monument's 20 culturally-associated American Indian tribes consider them sacred sites.

Location:	Established:
Harpers Ferry, IA	1949

Fort Larned National Historic Site

As settlers pushed west through the Southern Plains American Indian territory, there were many conflicts. Raiding was common along the Santa Fe Trail. Fort Larned was founded in 1859 to protect the settlers and others traveling from the eastern part of the United States. It was designated a National Historic Site more than a hundred years later.

Company A of the 10th, an African-American Calvary unit, served here. African-American regiments deserted and drank less than traditional army units, but they faced bigotry. When their stables were burned and horses killed, no investigation was made. Instead, authorities sent them to a different fort.

Location:	Established:
Larned, KS	1964

Belle of Louisville **National Historic Landmark**

Built in 1914, *Belle of Louisville* is the oldest operating steamboat of her kind in the nation, propelled by a 17-foot (5.2-meter) paddlewheel. The original seven-foot (2.13-meter) maple wheel with a steam-powered steering system operated with a brass stick that sits in front.

Just before the Kentucky Derby each year, *Belle of Louisville* races another steamboat on the Ohio River. There are no rules and the only prize is a pair of gilded antlers, which the winning boat mounts on its forecastle.

Location:	Established:
Louisville, KY	1989

Poverty Point National Monument

Hunter-gatherers rarely constructed large-scale monuments, but evidence at Poverty Point suggests they did at least once. It is an engineering marvel, the product of millions of hours of labor, and seems related to a vast, ancient trading network. It's a UNESCO World Heritage Site.

The grave of a human from the 1200s was found about 150 miles (240 kilometers) from this monument. He was buried with charms within a medicine bundle, with ancient artifacts from the Poverty Point mounds, indicating he must have valued the artifacts found there.

Location:	Established:
Pioneer, LA	1962

Fort Western National Historic Landmark

Built in 1754, Fort Western is the oldest log fort in the United States. British colonists used it as a base to expand territory through North America. A fortified storehouse with a four-pound (1.81 kilogram) cannon, it supplied nearby Fort Halifax.

Benedict Arnold used Fort Western as a staging point for his assault on Quebec in 1775 during the American Revolution. He stayed about a week as his supplies were loaded. Some of Arnold's officers, including Aaron Burr, Alexander Hamilton's killer, also stayed nearby.

Location:	Established:
Augusta, ME	1973

Maryland

Harriet Tubman Underground Railroad National Historical Park

Harriet Tubman is the Underground Railroad's best-known conductor, helping hundreds of slaves to freedom. Free blacks, abolitionists, and church leaders assisted. Tubman traveled from Maryland to Ontario and back, often carrying a rifle for protection and to ensure escapees didn't reconsider.

During the Civil War, Tubman served the United States Army as a spy, scout, nurse, and cook and received military recognition at her burial. Yet in life, she was denied military pension until she finally won a small sum through years of protest and struggle with the U.S. government.

Location:	Established:
Church Creek, MD	2013

Massachusetts

Salem Maritime National Historic Site

Salem's historic buildings, wharves, and reconstructed tall ships tell of the sailors, Revolutionary War privateers, and merchants who helped

(Massachusetts continued)

distribute goods to a growing America. Its private homes contain the histories of people who lived through more than three centuries of American industrialization.

One of the private homes had trash pits containing years of food garbage—the perfect artifacts to study historic diets. From the remains, archaeologists found that in addition to the common meats of today, diners enjoyed bullfrog, gull, passenger pigeon, and Canada goose.

Location:	Established:
Salem, MA	1938

Michigan

Keweenaw Peninsula National Historic Park

In the mid-1800s, the invention of the telegraph, which used copper wires, started "copper fever." Copper mining was an enduring industry in the remote Keweenaw Peninsula for more than a hundred years.

Miners started as young men, knowing the risk of death. One named Frank said, "Men meant nothing. …When somebody got killed years ago in the mine there, you would hear the whistle, not very loud, just a mourning [sound]…[and] somebody would run to the Captain's office to ask for the job."

Location:	Established:
Kalumet, MI	1992

Grand Portage National Monument

This was a meeting place for American Indians and fur traders, an essential link between the waterways of the Arctic and Atlantic Oceans. Ojibwe traveled from summer homes on Lake Superior to winter hunting grounds in the interior of Minnesota and Ontario.

Seeds were among the objects traded. Indians traded beans, corn, and squash to the settlers for peas and parsnips, which were new to them. Because growers kept seeds from each harvest year to year, the same 200-year-old vegetable varieties are still being grown.

Location:	Established:
Grand Portage, MN	1960

Natchez National Historical Park

American Indians cultivated crops here, making earthen mounds as part of their civic centers. French and Spanish traders and explorers clashed with the natives; eventually the area was home to southern plantation owners, slaves, and free blacks.

William Johnson, a free black, became a successful barber, teacher, and business owner and father of eleven. He kept a detailed diary of his life from 1835 to 1851, the year a neighbor shot him. Though a freed slave, he owned sixteen slaves of his own and wrote about the difficulties of slave ownership.

Location:	Established:
Natchez, MS	1988

Fort Osage National Historic Landmark

This fort was built on the Missouri River under the direction of William Clark, of the Lewis and Clark Expedition. A military garrison and trading center, it meant to keep good relations with the Osage natives. The fort provided defense against the British, Spanish, and French military.

The Osage were hunters and gatherers who made a strong impression because of their size. According to one observer, they were nearly giants and many were more than six feet (1.83 meters) tall, which was rare in those days.

Location:	Established:
Sibley, MO	1972

★★★★★★★★ Montana ★★★★★★★★

Little Bighorn Battlefield National Monument

The Battle of the Little Bighorn pitted Lieutenant Colonel Custer's troops against Lakota Sioux and Cheyenne warriors who fought to stay on native lands. Known

(Montana continued)
as Custer's Last Stand, 3,000 natives commanded by Sitting Bull overwhelmed Custer's 600 troops.

The U.S. government broke treaties with the Sioux and Cheyenne because of the quest for gold in South Dakota's Black Hills. The betrayal was the last straw: more than 10,000 American Indians gathered on the Little Bighorn River, which they called Greasy Grass, to resist.

Location:	Established:
Crow Agency, MT	1946

Nebraska

Homestead National Monument

Abraham Lincoln's Homestead Act of 1862 gave free land to almost everyone: men, women, immigrants, and, by 1868, African Americans. People established homesteads of 160 acres (64.75 hectares), eventually spreading into 30 states and a total of 270 million acres (109,265,123.41 hectares).

Daniel Freeman was one of the first to file a homestead claim. When he moved to Nebraska, he corresponded with his late brother's fiancée, who eventually married Freeman. Together they had eight children and were cornerstones in the community.

Location:	Established:
Beatrice, NE	1936

Gold Butte National Monument

This national monument is nearly 300,000 acres (121,405.69 hectares). It offers natural features and cultural history. The sculpted red sandstone and twisting canyons provide stunning vistas. Ancient rock art and rock shelters, hearths, and agave roasting pits are part of the American Indian cultural heritage.

The Mojave Desert tortoise, a threatened species, lives here. About a foot long, this tortoise has a very small chance of survival into adulthood, but once it's made it past its first few years of life, it is likely to live between 50 and 80 years.

Location:	Established:
Clark County, NV	2016

Harrisville National Historic Landmark District

In the early years of the Industrial Revolution, mill towns like Harrisville were key employers and producers of textiles. The isolated rural setting of Harrisville has allowed it to stay true to its original form, partly due to the long-running operation of Cheshire Mills.

As much as 45 percent of the local village population worked for the mills. They were carders, spinners, dyers, weavers, finishers, and mechanics. Other members of the community supplied wool for spinning, wood for the boilers, and food.

Location:	Established:
Harrisville, NH	1977

Thomas Edison National Historical Park

Thomas Edison is best known for inventing the electric lightbulb, but he also designed a system of power plants that made the power and the wiring that brought it to people's homes. His home and laboratories contain archives and artifacts from his thousands of inventions.

Though Edison was very hard of hearing, he was fascinated by the idea of recording human voice. In 1877, he recorded himself reading a nursery rhyme on a piece of tin foil, and played it back on the phonograph he invented.

Location:	Established:
West Orange, NJ	1966

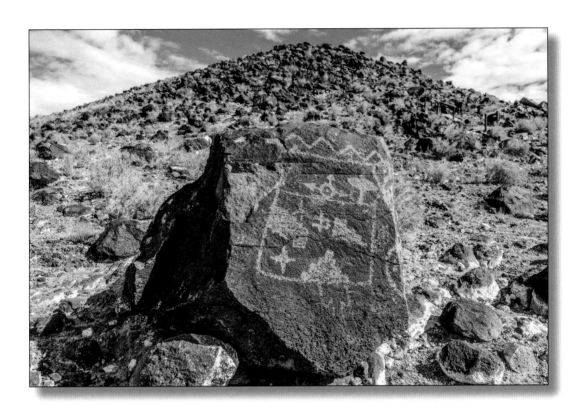

Petroglyph National Monument

This monument preserves one of the largest petroglyph concentrations in North America, containing more than 25,000 highly fragile petroglyphs. The images are pecked into dark boulders along volcanic cliffs and possess deep spiritual significance for today's Pueblo Indians and other native people.

Many of the area's native plants have been used as medicine. To soothe a cough, ground Apache Plume roots is mixed with sugar, while the green berries of horse nettle were crushed, mixed with salt, and bound to the throat to treat enlarged tonsils.

Location:	Established:
Albuquerque, NM	1990

Seneca Falls Women's Rights National Historical Park

The women's movement began here with a large convention on women's rights in 1848. Along with the meeting site, visitors can tour the homestead of Elizabeth Cady Stanton, a key organizer and lifelong women's rights advocate.

Stanton, a married mother of seven, had a 50-year friendship with Susan B. Anthony, who was unmarried and free to travel. Anthony helped keep house while Stanton wrote the speeches. They joked that they worked out disputes, power struggles, and equal rights in the household as well as the nation.

Location:	Established:
Seneca Falls, NY	1980

North Carolina

Cape Hatteras Lighthouse Station

The Cape Hatteras Lighthouse protects one of the most hazardous sections of the Atlantic Coast. Hundreds of shipwrecks in this area have given it the reputation as the

(North Carolina continued)

Graveyard of the Atlantic. It is the tallest brick lighthouse in the United States at almost 200 feet (60.96 meters).

Each lighthouse has a distinct paint pattern known as a daymark, which allows sailors to recognize it during daylight among others along the coast. The light sequence, called nightmark, does the same at night.

Location:	Established:
Buxton, NC	1937

North Dakota

Knife River Indian Village National Historic Site

Hidatsa women owned and built the large, circular earth-lodge dwellings called awahte. An older, experienced woman supervised the building process. The finished earth lodge was between 30 and 60 feet (9–18 meters) wide and ten to 15 feet (3–4.6 meters) high. Sisters and their families lived there in groups.

The Lewis and Clark Expedition befriended and traded with the people of the Mandan and Hidatsa earth-lodge villages while wintering here in 1804–05, gaining knowledge about the territory ahead. They met Sacagawea, the Shoshone woman who would serve as a guide on the expedition.

Location:	Established:
Stanton, ND	1974

Ohio

★ ★ ★ ★ ★ ★ ★ ★ ★ ★ ★ ★ ★ ★ ★ ★

Charles Young Buffalo Soldiers National Monument

The first African American to reach the rank of colonel in the
U.S. Army, Charles Young was also the first national park
superintendent, of Sequoia and General Grant National Parks.
The child of slaves, he commanded the African-American regiment
known as the Buffalo Soldiers.

An all African-American Army regiment, the Buffalo Soldiers were
nicknamed by American Indians due to their fierce fighting and their
dark, curly hair. Though they only earned $13 a day, they were treated
with more dignity in the military than in civilian life.

Location:	Established:
Wilberforce, OH	2013

Oklahoma

Washita Battlefield National Historic Site

In 1868, the 7th U.S. Cavalry, led by Lt. Colonel Custer, attacked the winter encampment of Southern Cheyenne. Their leader, Black Kettle, had sought protection from the U.S. Army, signing two treaties prior to the attack. He and his wife, Medicine Woman Later, were gunned down in the attack.

General Philip H. Sheridan planned the attack during the winter. He knew the Cheyenne warriors depended on their horses in battle, and tended to fight in the spring and summer, when the horses were strongest from eating grass. In winter the horses had less feed, and weren't as strong.

Location:	Established:
Cheyenne, OK	1965

35

Oregon Caves National Monument

Hidden within the Siskiyou Mountains, the Oregon Caves is unusual because it is formed in marble. Its passages run for about 15,000 feet (4,572 meters). Rare fossils have been found there, including a grizzly bear more than 50,000 years old and a jaguar fossil between 40,000 and 20,000 years old.

Early opportunists tried schemes to make money from the Oregon Caves. In the 1890s, Alfonso B. Smith made exaggerated claims, saying a horse and buggy could drive through ten miles (16 kilometers) of the caves and that he planned to build a transportation device like a streetcar within it, all of which were false. He eventually disappeared.

Location:	Established:
Cave Junction, OR	1909

Pennsylvania

Gettysburg National Military Park

More than 50,000 soldiers were killed, wounded, or captured during the three day Battle of Gettysburg, making it the site of the largest battle ever waged in

(Pennsylvania continued)
the Western Hemisphere. Confederate General Robert E. Lee was defeated as he tried to invade the North, marking a turning point in the Civil War.

Boys as young as 16 took part in the Civil War. Some played the drums or the bugle. Their music communicated battle orders. The notes and beats of the instruments carried commands farther and quicker than humans could.

Location:	Established:
Gettysburg, PA	1895

 # Rhode Island

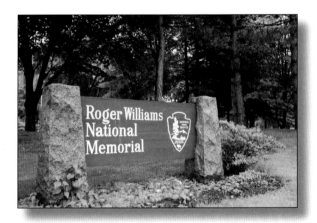

Roger Williams National Memorial Park

In the 1600s, Roger Williams was driven from the colonies because he supported religious freedom and thought it was wrong to take land belonging to American Indians. He and his followers purchased land in Narragansett Bay from the Narragansett Indians. It became Rhode Island, a haven for Baptists, Quakers, Jews, and other religious minorities.

Nearly a century after his death, Williams's notion of a "wall of separation" between church and state inspired Thomas Jefferson and James Madison, who incorporated it into the U.S. Constitution and Bill of Rights.

Location:	Established:
Providence, RI	1965

South Carolina

Fort Sumter
National Monument

On April 11, 1861, Major Robert Anderson, pro-slavery but a Union military man, occupied Fort Sumter with his men. Confederate Brig. General Pierre Beauregard demanded surrender. The Union held until the next day, when the officer's quarters were burned. Anderson declared a truce, but the Civil War had begun.

After Major Anderson's surprising stand, the American flag was charged with new meaning. Since men were fighting to preserve the Union, it had more significance. Previously only used for ceremony, it was now seen flying from houses, stores, churches, and above the village greens and college quads.

Location:	Established:
Charleston, SC	1948

South Dakota

Jewel Cave
National Monument

Frank and Albert Michaud found a hole into the cave, which they blasted with dynamite. Inside, they discovered crawlways and low-ceilinged rooms coated

(South Dakota continued)

with beautiful calcite crystals, which appeared like jewels. They filed a mining claim, but hoped to make money by attracting visitors. They even organized the "Jewel Cave Dancing Club" in 1902 to attract tourists.

A geologist named Dwight Deal came along and enlisted the help of two rock climbing adventurers, Herb and Jan Conn. Together they explored and mapped new passages, eventually upwards of 15 miles (24 kilometers) within Jewel Cave.

Location:	Established:
Custer, SD	1908

★ ★ ★ ★ ★ ★ ★ ★ ★ Tennessee ★ ★ ★ ★ ★ ★ ★ ★ ★

Wynnewood State Historic Site
National Historic Landmark

Eons ago, mammoths and smaller game came here for the mineral salt deposited. Eventually a spa was built, offering sulfur water cures for skin problems, indigestion, and liver disease. By 1830, it was a major stagecoach rest stop on the route into Tennessee. The Wynne family farmed for more than 140 years.

Thomas Sharp Spencer, a larger than life hunter, lived during the winter between 1778–1779 in a giant sycamore tree near the mineral salt lick. According to legend, American Indians were fearful of his large stature and enormous footprints.

Location:	Established:
Castalian Springs, TN	1972

Waco Mammoth National Monument

In 1978, two fossil and arrowhead hunters discovered the bone of a Columbian mammoth near the Bosque River. When archaeologists excavated, they found the fossils of 16 Columbian mammoths. Later, six more were found, along with the remains of a camel and the tooth of a saber-tooth cat.

Nineteen mammoths from a nursery herd died together about 65,000 years ago. They were not killed by predators but trapped in a steep-sided channel, and likely drowned in a flood. Three others died in a similar manner about 15,000 years later.

Location:	Established:
Waco, TX	2015

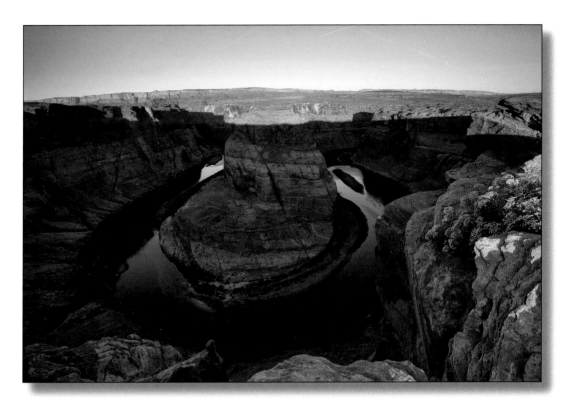

Grand Staircase-Escalante National Monument

This nearly two million square acre area contains natural, cultural, and archaeological significance. Evidence of native people is found in remaining rock art and ruins. Dinosaur fossils over 75 million years old have been found, including one 30 feet (9 meters) long with a powerful jaw containing more than 800 teeth.

In 1879, Mormons traveled through the southeast corner of Utah. At the nearly impassable cliffs around Glen Canyon, they used explosives to enlarge a crevice to go forward. On the east side of the river, a maze of canyons, mesas, and cliffs made the area almost impassible.

Location:	Established:
Kanab, UT	1996

Mount Independence National Historic Landmark

This site fortified Lake Champlain to defend against British attacks from the North during the American Revolutionary War. American, British, and German forces occupied the fort, houses, and hospital alternately during the hostilities. After the war, the land was used for farming.

Chert, or flint, was useful to natives as arrowhead and tools, while the Americans made gunflints. The Americans also found sulfur nearby, which they used for both medicine and making gunpowder.

Location:	Established:
Orwell, VT	1972

Booker T. Washington National Monument

Born a slave to a single mother, Booker T. Washington was freed at age nine. He worked his way through college. The first principal at the African American Tuskegee Institute, his life's work was to lift African Americans out of poverty and social limitation using education and peaceful negotiation with the ruling classes.

Washington was criticized for working with politicians and aiming for education rather than militant approach. But secretly he supported court challenges to segregation and restrictions on voter registration, giving money to the National Association for the Advancement of Colored People (NAACP) for these purposes.

Location:	Established:
Hardy, VA	1956

Mount St. Helens National Volcanic Monument

This volcano's eruption in 1980 was the most destructive in U.S. history. The magma spread over 230 square miles (596 square kilometers), flattening vegetation and covering buildings. Fifty-seven people died and many homes, bridges, railways, and highways were destroyed. Nearly 7,000 big game animals such as deer, elk, and bear died.

A Klickitat tribe legend says that Mount St. Helens was originally a maiden loved by two brothers. Their war over her collapsed a huge bridge, creating the Columbia River Gorge cascades. As punishment, the chief turned his sons into two mountains: Mount Hood and Mount Adams, and their beloved into Mount St. Helens.

Location:	Established:
Mt. St. Helens, WA	1982

Belmont-Paul Women's Equality National Monument

This has been the home of the National Woman's Party (NWP) since 1929. It's where Alice Paul led the NWP to target Congress and the White House through sustained dramatic, nonviolent protest. They marched, sang, faced violence and arrest, went on hunger strikes and finally won the vote in 1920.

In 1923, Alice Paul introduced the Equal Rights Amendment (ERA), an amendment to the United States Constitution guaranteeing equal rights for women. Congress passed the ERA in 1972 but, to date, it remains three states short of ratification. For more than fifty years, the ERA has been introduced in every session of Congress.

Location:	Established:
Capitol Hill, Washington, D.C.	1974

West Virginia

Harpers Ferry National Historic Park

John Brown attempted a raid on the armory here in 1859 to start a slave revolt. He thought slaves in the area would join in. While his plan didn't work—and most everyone involved was either killed or hanged—he was later considered a hero in the abolitionist movement.

Brown's men shot a railroad porter, Hayward Shepherd. The noise alerted Dr. John Starry who was confronted by Brown's men. When Starry said he couldn't help Shepherd, Brown's men allowed him to leave. Starry alerted the town about the raid, ultimately bringing about the capture of Brown's men.

Location:	Established:
Harpers Ferry, WV	1963

Wisconsin

Fountain Lake Farm National Historic Landmark

This was John Muir's boyhood farm, where he fell in love with the woods, meadows, and lake, beginning a lifetime of dedication to the natural world. He was considered the father of the National Park Service and he founded the Sierra Club.

(Wisconsin continued)

John Muir knew that taking President Theodore Roosevelt camping in Yosemite would be a huge boost to protecting special natural places across the country. He was right: Roosevelt signed into existence five national parks, 18 national monuments, 51 national bird sanctuaries and wildlife refuges, and more than 100 million acres of national forests.

Location:	Established:
Montello, WI	1990

Wyoming

Devil's Tower National Monument

This volcanic monolith became the first national monument when it was brought to the attention of Theodore Roosevelt. It's made of igneous rock and towers dramatically 1,267 feet (386 meters) above the surrounding terrain. Twenty-seven Native tribes are associated with Devil's Tower.

In 1941, George Hopkins, a professional parachutist, was dropped by airplane on the top of the tower along with a rope with which he planned to descend. When the rope landed out of reach, he was stuck there for six days until a rescue party climbed up to get him.

Location:	Established:
Hulett, WY	1906

Index

Admiralty Island National Monument 5

Belle of Louisville National
Historic Landmark 19

Belmont-Paul Women's Equality
National Monument 45

Booker T Washington
National Monument 43

Brown Chapel AME Church
National Historic Landmark 4

Canyon de Chelly National Monument 6

Cape Hatteras Light House Station 32

Castillo de San Marcos
National Monument 12

Charles Young Buffalo Soldiers
National Monument 34

Devil's Tower National Monument 47

Duck Creek Aqueduct National
Historic Landmark 16

Effigy Mounds National Monument 17

Fort Larned National Historic Site 18

Fort Osage National Historic Landmark 36

Fort Sumter National Monument 28

Fort Western National
Historic Landmark 21

Fountain Lake Farm National
Historic Landmark 46

Gettysburg National Military Park 36

Gold Butte National Monument 28

Grand Portage National Monument 44

Grand Staircase-Escalante
National Monument 41

Hagerman Horse Fossil Beds National
Monument 15

Harpers Ferry National
Historic Park 46

Harriet Tubman Underground Railroad
National Historical Park 22

Harrisville National Historic Landmark
District 29

Homestead National Monument 37

Jewel Cave National Monument 28

Keweenaw Peninsula National Historic
Park 23

Knife River Indian Village National
Historic Site 33

Little Bighorn Battlefield
National Monument 26

Little Rock Central High School National
Historic Site 7

Manzanar National Historic Site 8

Mount Independence National Historic
Landmark 42

Mount St. Helens National
Volcanic Monument 44

Natchez National Historical Park 25

New Castle Courthouse Museum National
Historic Landmark 11

Ocmulgee National Monument 13

Oregon Caves National Monument 36

Papahanaumokua Kea Marine
National Monument 14

Petroglyph National Monument 31

Poverty Point National Monument 20

Pullman National Monument 16

Roger Williams National Memorial
Park 37

Salem Maritime National Historic Site 22

Sand Creek Massacre
National Historic Site 9

Seneca Falls Women's Rights
National Historical Park 32

Thomas Edison National Historical Park 30

Waco Mammoth National Monument 40

Washita Battlefield National
Historic Site 35

Weir Farm National Historic Site 10

Wynnewood State Historic Site 39

www.rourkeeducationalmedia.com

PHOTO CREDITS: Alaska © Arun123, Arizona © Benny Marty; California © Christopher Boswell, Connecticut © Nancy Kennedy; Florida monument co and page 12 © Sean Pavone; Georgia © Jeffrey M. Frank; Kentucky © Thomas Kelley; Massachusetts © sanya51; Michigan © ehrlif; Minnesota Monu cover and page 24 © Rajesh Pattabiraman; Montana © Don Mammoser; Nebraska © Weldon Schloneger; Nevada monument cover and page 28 © kenkistler; New Hampshire © LEE SNIDER PHOTO IMAGES; New jersey © Joseph Sohm; New Mexico © turtix; New York Monument cover and page © Zack Frank; North Carolina cover and page 32 © Pi-Lens; Pennsylvania © Felix Lipov; Rhode Island © Jeffrey M. Frank; South Carolina © SKPG_Ar Utah © Bill45; Washington © The Adaptive; West Virginia © Andrei Medvedev; Wyoming © David Harmantas; All photos from Sutterstock.com except: Alabama © © James Kirkikis | Dreamstime.com, Arkansas © Adam Jones, Ph.D. https://creativecommons.org/licenses/by-sa/3.0/deed.en , Colorado chapin31 - istockphoto; Delaware © Ataraxy22 https://creativecommons.org/licenses/by-sa/3.0/deed.en ; Hawaii © courtesy of NOAA; Idaho © Dade Illinois © © Jim Roberts | Dreamstime.com; Indiana courtesy of the Library of Congress; Kansas courtesy of Nathan King / National Park Service; Louisiana Image Courtesy of Louisiana State Parks; Maine © Billy Hathorn https://creativecommons.org/licenses/by-sa/3.0/deed.en ; Maryland © Herb Quick / Alamy Stock Photo; Minnesota © © Stevengaertner | Dreamstime.com; Mississippi © Anne Power | Dreamstime.com; Missouri © Americasro https://creativecommons.org/licenses/by-sa/2.5/deed.en ; North Dakota © Xerxes2004 https://creativecommons.org/licenses/by-sa/3.0/ ; Ohio © Nytte Oklahoma © Patrick Jay https://creativecommons.org/licenses/by-sa/3.0/deed.en ; Oregon courtesy of the National Park Service; South Dakota © https://creativecommons.org/licenses/by-sa/2.0/deed.en; Tennessee © E. Patrick McIntyre, Jr., Tennessee Historical Commission, Nashville, TN. Texas © Larry D. Moore https://creativecommons.org/licenses/by-sa/3.0/deed.en; Vermont © Zeph77 https://creativecommons.org/licenses/by-sa/3.0 deed.en ; Virginia © MarmadukePercy https://creativecommons.org/licenses/by-sa/3.0/deed.en ; Washington D.C. © AgnosticPreachersKid https:// creativecommons.org/licenses/by-sa/3.0/deed.en ; Wisconsin © Royalbroil on en.wikipedia https://creativecommons.org/licenses/by-sa/2.5/deed.en

Edited by: Keli Sipperley   Cover and Interior design by: Nicola Stratford   www.nicolastratford.com

Library of Congress PCN Data

HISTORIC MONUMENTS / Linden McNeilly
(STATE GUIDES)
    ISBN 978-1-68342-402-4 (hard cover)
    ISBN 978-1-68342-472-7 (soft cover)
    ISBN 978-1-68342-568-7 (e-Book)
Library of Congress Control Number: 2017931408

Printed in the United States of America, North Mankato, Minnesota